Hello New!

edited by John Agard

illustrated by Lydia Monks

ORCHARD BOOKS

Hello New!

To the memory of Ted Hughes
– for his nurturing respect for children's writing
– and his celebration of
"the little goblin in a word".

J.A.

For Anna-Marie, Rebecca and Julie.

L.M.

Orchard Books
96 Leonard Street, London EC2A 4XD
Orchard Books Australia
Unit 31/56 O'Riordan Street, Alexandria, NSW 2015
ISBN 1 84121 621 6 (hardback)
ISBN 1 84362 094 4 (paperback)
First published in Great Britain in 2000
First paperback publication in 2002
This selection © John Agard 2000
Illustrations © Lydia Monks 2000
The rights of John Agard to be identified as the compiler and
Lydia Monks to be identified as the illustrator have been
asserted by them in accordance with the
Copyright, Designs and Patents Act, 1988.
A CIP catalogue record for this book
is available from the British Library
1 3 5 7 9 10 8 6 4 2 (hardback)
1 3 5 7 9 10 8 6 4 2 (paperback)
Printed in Great Britain

A Word from John Agard...

One word can be a springboard into a poem.

One word can get the imagination going.

Here it was the word 'New'.

To all poets a big thank you for taking the leap

and landing on their feet

with a new poem.

Thanks also to Juliet Nolan and Francesca Dow

for their enthusiasm and

for keeping things on course.

Now it's over to you, the reader.

Hello, you! What's new?

contents

Contents

Contents

Contents

smiles like Roses

by Helen Dunmore

All down my street
smiles opened like roses
Sun licked me and tickled me
Sun said, *Didn't you believe me*
when I said I'd be back?

I blinked my eyes, I said,
Sun, you are too strong for me
where'd you get those muscles?
Sun said, *Come and dance.*

All over the park
smiles opened like roses
babies kicked off their shoes
and sun kissed their toes.

All those new babies
all that new sun
everybody dancing
walking but dancing.

All over the world
Sun kicked off his shoes
and came home dancing
licking and tickling

kissing crossing-ladies and fat babies
saying to everyone
Hey you are the most beautiful
dancing people I've ever seen
with those smiles like roses!

A New Blue Bike

by JOHN RICE

It's the first day of Spring.

A girl and two boys
are mending a puncture.

The weak sun spikes the water
in the basin
and the bubbles from
the submerged inner tube
rise up like tiny balls.

Spanners, oil can, repair kit,
spoons and screwdrivers all lie
on the pavement,
warming their winter metal.

A girl and two boys
are mending a puncture
under a thin cloud,
beside nodding daffodils.

A new blue bike for a new yellow year.

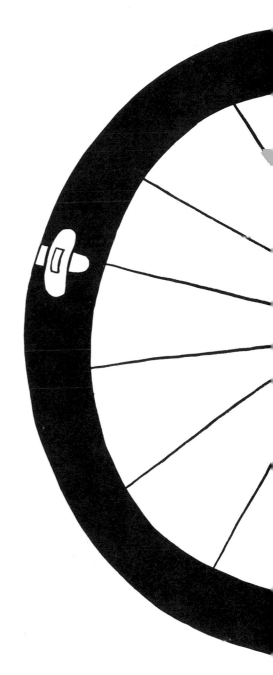

Archibald, Marjorie, and Otto: Cuckoo!

by MARK HEWITT

Archibald Spratt
Wore a cat for a hat
Which he stuck to his head with glue;
On the first day of Spring
He would walk round in rings
Shouting, "God Save the King"
WHAT'S NEW?

Marjorie Sugg
Cleaned her teeth with a slug
That was taped to the end of a screw;
On the first day of Spring
She would sprout lovely wings
And fly off to Beijing
WHAT'S NEW?

Otto van Krantz
Kept red ants in his pants
And fed them with apples and stew;
On the first day of Spring
He would buy lots of string
And tie it round things
WHAT'S NEW?

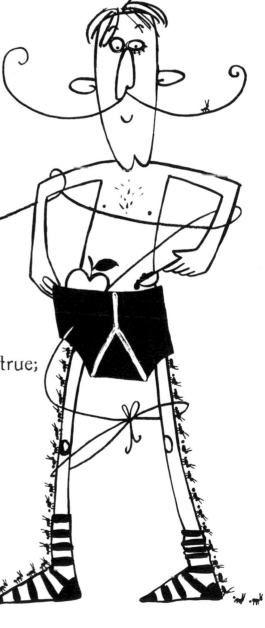

The first day of Spring,
Oh, the first day of Spring,
There's no day more wondrous, it's true;
When that sparky mad zing
Hits you like a bee sting
There's no choice but to sing
HALLOO?
HALLOO?
And go totally cuckoo
WHAT'S NEW?

The Rain's Feet

by GEORGE SZIRTES

The rain is slowly ticking over, then it picks up speed.
I can hear its tiny feet running every which way.

Why is it in such a hurry? It has the whole day
in front of it. And every new footstep is a new lead.

After the Storm

by OPAL PALMER ADISA

After the rain has fallen
as if God had been dumping
gigantic buckets of water
I run outside
where puddles have formed
and splash around.

The world seems especially clean.
I twirl around.
I jump over rainbows.
I stomp real hard.
Mud splatters my clothes
in intricate designs.

Mother calls me in
Scolds me all the way to the bathroom.

After I have taken my bath
I peer through the window
loving this new world
washed clean by God's water.

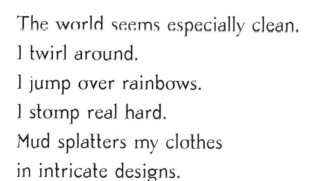

The Mucky Princess

by ADRIAN MITCHELL

The mucky princess
liked to play in the mud
she would wallow and roll and dig

The mucky princess
loved the mud so much
she found a new job as a pig

Before the Ball

by JOHN AGARD

Fairy godmother

O there you are
with your magic wand
and here's a pumpkin
I picked with my own hand.

Wow. How do you do it?
A golden coach just like that!
And that fancy coachman –
was he really a rat?

And those upright footmen –
no one can tell
they are leaping frogs
you've dressed in a spell.

And those six white horses
bedecked so nice —
can they remember their days
as six white mice?

Even my old ash-rags
you've turned to finery.
Bet my sisters
won't recognize me.

But one last thing please
before you go.
O fairy godmother
don't think I'm a bother

but these new slippers
are pinching my toe.

Roses Round My Door

by Geraldine McCaughrean

I planted roses round my door:
It sounded so romantic.
Now I can't get out no more:
I'm inside, going frantic.

They came in through the letter box
And bounded up the staircase;
I feel like blooming Goldilocks
Trapped in that clawful bears' place.

Peace hybrids snooze on the new settee;
Dog-roses drove out Rover;
Tea blooms are sitting down to tea:
The roses have taken over!

Fetch a ladder! Fetch an axe!
Call the rose-red Fire Brigade!
Planting roses round my door
Was the worst mistake I ever made.

Three

by CAROL ANN DUFFY

I met a miniature King
by the side of the road,
wearing a crown
and an ermine suit —
important, small,
plump as a natterjack toad,
Kneel! he shrieked, *Kneel for the King!*
CERTAINLY not, I said,
I'll do no such thing.

I saw a Giantess,
tall as a tree.
You'll do for a new doll, she bellowed,
just the toy for me!
Into the box! Scream hard! Scream long!
I stared at her mad, pond eyes
then skipped away.
Dream on…

I bumped into Invisible Boy - *ouch!* –
at the edge of the field.
Give me a chocolate drop
said a voice.
What do you say?
Please.
So I did
then stared as it floated mid-air
and melted away.

These are three of the people I met yesterday.

Broomstick Ballet

by JOHN AGARD

My bristles brave your dust
till floor is swept clean.
Then I am left to lean
against kitchen wall.
Just a broom. That's all
I am to you. But you're wrong.

Head-up and all serene
I do my one-leg pirouette.
Such grace you've never seen.
Yes, I'm a prima donna
In my out-of-sight corner
And I repeat, lest you forget,

Your new vacuum cleaner
is a mere onlooker
to the world of broomstick ballet.

Haven't a clue

by DAVE CALDER

What will it be?
Don't ask me.
Thin or fat?
I don't know that.
Short or tall?
I can't say at all.
Brown eyes or blue?
Haven't a clue.
A dreamer, a screamer?
I've no idea, dear.
I can only tell you
that it will be new
and that certainly
nothing will be
quite the same
again

Welcome Wishes to two New Babies

(for Zoe and Lola)

by ADRIAN MITCHELL

the milk of the moon
the wine of the sun
the friendship of grass
and salty sand

adventures with Jumblies
and Peter Rabbit
and all the daft creatures
of Wonderland

Paul, Ringo,
George and John
bless the floors
you dance upon

elephant rides
affectionate apes
and the sheep and rocks
of mountainside farms

a cat which will curl
round your neck like a scarf
and a golden retriever
to lie in your arms

I wish you wild happy and gentle sad
and all the love of your Mum and Dad

Seventeen Things to do With a Baby

(for Paul Lawrence Hackett)

by JUDITH NICHOLLS

Watch
his eyes
watch your eyes,
search out his mother's face,
follow other faces;
wonder who he'll recognize.

Feel
his fingers
monkey-grip your finger,
feet frog-kick against your hand;
wonder when he'll stand.

Talk to him!
Chatter, recite, hum!
Watch his tongue curl,
lips part and close;
he knows already
how to listen.
Whistle, whisper, say anything;
sing him a nursery-rhyme
and wonder when, one day,
he'll start to sing.

Listen!
He sucks like any new-born calf
or toddler with his first straw,
unwilling to stop;
wonder when he'll drain his cup
eagerly to the final, noisy drop.

Wonder.

The Thing

by GARETH OWEN

Something crept in with the moon last night
A thing
This new thing in our house
And it wasn't a cat and it wasn't a dog
And it certainly wasn't a mouse
This thing
No it certainly wasn't a mouse.

It must be an alien, I thought to myself
This thing
Yes an alien, that's what it must be
That flew through the dark in a silver ship
At midnight silently
This thing
By starlight secretly.

I could tell it was trying to speak to me
This thing
To speak through the bedroom wall
But it spoke in a language of gurgles and shouts
That made no sense at all
This thing
No it made no sense at all.

I had to find out what it looked like
This thing
This thing in Mum's room next door
So I crept down the hallway and into her room
And there by her side I saw
This thing
This thing is what I saw.

'Oh, Mum,' I said, 'what is it
That thing
With its face all wrinkled and red?'
And she smiled and placed its fist in mine

'Meet your new little sister,' she said
She said
'Meet your lovely new sister,' she said.

Who Wants to be a Dragonfly?

by LAURENCE LERNER

When you were still a little child,
How gradually you grew;
At 13 you got hairier
And taller: that was new.
You thought, Is this strange person
Still me? It can't be true.

Time passed (for that's the only thing
That time is sure to do,
Just as birds are sure to sing
And cows are sure to moo,
Just as trains to France are sure
To start from Waterloo).

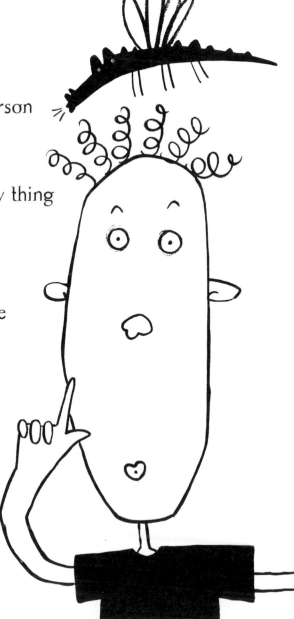

Your body is a kind of ship:
The arms and legs are crew,
The heart supplies the energy
That powers all you do.
Your eyes are searchlights so you'll know
Where you are going to.

Turtles live for years and years,
Cats live for just a few;
Dragonflies are born and die
After a day or two.
Who wants to be a dragonfly?
Not me, I'm sure. Do you?

Kicking through the New

(for Kalera)

by GRACE NICHOLS

Learning to swim –
your land-accustomed girl-walking body
turns horizontal-wriggly,

Arms and legs such strange things,
like wayward paddling fins,
trying to get you from A to B to C,

And yes you're learning how to be –
a submarine dancer
a froggie
a floatie
a spirogyra

Kicking through the new,
yet familiar
element – called water.

What's New?

by JOHN MOLE

*Haven't you grown
says my Gran
since I last saw you.
Oh my very own
not so little man,
how I adore you!*

She doesn't half
go on. Every time
it's the same old spiel
and they all laugh
politely, and I'm
supposed to as well.

I mean, I don't ever
tell her *Granny, oh
you've started to shrink!*
No I'd never never
dream of it, no,
but that's what I think.

Perhaps when she's
much older
(when I am too)
then just for a tease
I'll tap her on the shoulder
and ask *What's new?*

old Tongue

by JACKIE KAY

When I was eight, I was forced south.
Not long after, when I opened
my mouth, a strange thing happened.
I lost my Scottish accent,
Words fell off my tongue:
eedyit, dreich, wabbit, crabbit
stummer, teuchter, heidbanger,
so you are, so am ur, see you, see ma ma,
shut yer geggie or I'll gie you the malkie!

My own vowels started to stretch like my bones
and I turned my back on Scotland.
Words disappeared in the dead of night,
new words marched in; ghastly, awful,
quite dreadful, *scones* said like *stones*.
Pokey hats into ice cream cones,
Oh where did all my words go –
my old words, my lost words?
Did you ever feel sad when you lost a word,
did you ever try and call it back
like calling in the sea.
If I could have found my words wandering,
I swear I would have taken them in,
swallowed them whole, knocked them back.

Out in the English soil, my old words
buried themselves. It made my mother's blood boil.
I cried one day with the wrong sound in my mouth.
I wanted them back; I wanted my old accent back,
my old tongue. My dour, soor Scottish tongue.
Sing-songy, I wanted to *gie it laldie.*

New Boy

by PETER SANSOM

He picked a fight with himself and split his lip.
He poked himself in the back with a protractor.
He told tales on himself.
He threw his coat in the girls' toilets.
He made himself laugh in assembly
       and got called to the front.

He nicked his maths book and wrote swearing all over it.
He nicked his ruler and wouldn't own up
        even though it had his initials on.
He flicked a rubber across the class and hit himself
        on the head.
He started bullying himself. No matter how early or late
        he was always there at the school gates.
He copied off himself. He got bad marks.
He kicked the back of his legs under the desk.
He drank his own milk while he wasn't looking.
He called himself names. "Hey four eyes"
        even though he didn't wear glasses.

I Love Johnnie Bake

by JOHN LYONS

I love Johnnie bake,
I love Johnnie bake.
My mout water
wen I think of Johnnie bake;
I in de kitchen
wen Granny make Johnnie bake.

Wen she grate coconut
to put in Johnnie bake
I eat de sweet, sweet bits
too small to grate.
She warn meh about belly ache;
but I cahn help it,
I really love Johnnie bake.

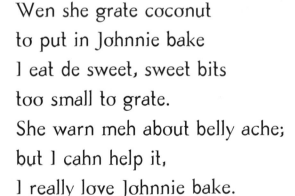

She kneading de flour
an she whole body shake.

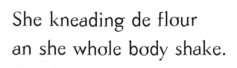

I near de oven,
where she bake Johnnie bake,
looking at how she cuff
de dough flat;
and I cahn get enough
of Johnnie bakes.
Nothing new!
I love Johnnie bake!
I LOVE JOHNNIE BAKE!

Glitterbread

by Brian Moses

I'm so bored with pitta bread
I want glitterbread.
Bread that gleams when it catches the light,
Bread that glows like the stars at night,
Bread that sparkles then starts to shimmer,
Bread that dazzles and never grows dimmer,
Bread that lights my way back home,
bread that shines like a precious stone.
I want glitterbread all the time,
Something new that's totally mine.

Keeping my own Company

by OPAL PALMER ADISA

I can't explain it
this new feeling
to wander off by myself
trekking through the woods
picking leaves and collecting twigs
listening to the chirping of birds and
the chatter of creatures.

Daddy says I've grown quiet
but he likes me just as much
this new me keeping my own company.

Mum says she sees me
really paying attention to things
and concludes I am maturing.

I don't know what it all means
but I like this new me more.
I'm my own best friend.

A Walk Through Yourself

by BRENDAN KENNELLY

Turn left at the crooked cross,
go straight over the bridge
where the brown river flows

to its own music,
past the bakery where bread
smells fresh at five in the morning.

To your left, the chapel among the trees
is peaceful as ever
and Molly Hagan in her house of love

is happy as a lark in spate.
The smell of apples from Bambury's orchard
whets your appetite

and when the castle soars into view
that tired feeling scuttles off,
you are a new man in a new time

ready to climb
one hundred and seven steps
to the top of the castle

and look out over the island
sitting there in the estuary,
a page of history, open and welcoming.

You contemplate the scene
and drink a little of its peace.
Then down the steps again

and hit the road for home.
There's Augustine Wallace in his wobbly car.
This is like walking through yourself,
enjoying whoever you are.

And who are you?

Drop a stone in the brown river.
Spot a lark in a singing tree.
Pick a companionable star.

New Book

by TONY MITTON

As you open its lid your mind unlocks.
The book itself is a brand new box.
And you pore that book by day and night,
For the book is a block of pure delight.
Then when you've done and the text is read
and your eyes are tired but your mind feels fed,
you may place that book on the silent shelf
but a bit of the book has become your new self.

The Magic of New Notebooks

by BILL LEWIS

I think I see one
just below the blank page,
like some fabulous creature
from the ocean depths.

I watch for a long time
but it does not rise.

I go away and come back.
Still no sign of movement.

I stir up the white water
with my biro. Suddenly
the poem bites at the nib.

I struggle with it for hours,
finally pulling it free.

I turn to the next page;
Pick up the pen and wait.
The new notebook is already
full of unwritten poems.

No Words to Forget

by IAN MCMILLAN

This poem
is so new
it's not
written yet

No lines
to remember
no words
to forget.

This poem
is so new
it's still
in my brain

It's waiting
to start
like a bus
or a train.

This poem
is so new
you could
write it yourself,

Then write
twenty more
to put
on your shelf!

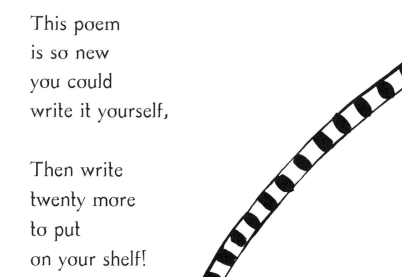

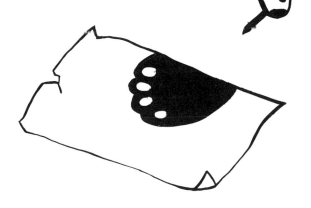

New Poem

by ROGER MCGOUGH

So far, so good.

But is there New in it?

by JOHN MOLE

A looking-glass with you in it,

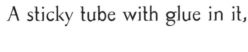

A sticky tube with glue in it,

A map with Timbuctoo in it,

An old box with a shoe in it,

A space-ship with a crew in it,

An owl with a tu-whoo in it,

A cage with a cockatoo in it,

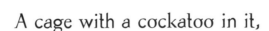

A cry with boo hoo hoo in it,

A kitten with a mew in it,

A paintbox with royal blue in it,

A sneeze with a kerchoo! in it,

A bathroom with shampoo in it,

A school hall with a queue in it,

A churchyard with a yew in it,

A band with a kazoo in it,

A poem with much ado in it . . .

Rhymes? There are quite a few in it,
And this last line has got NEW in it!

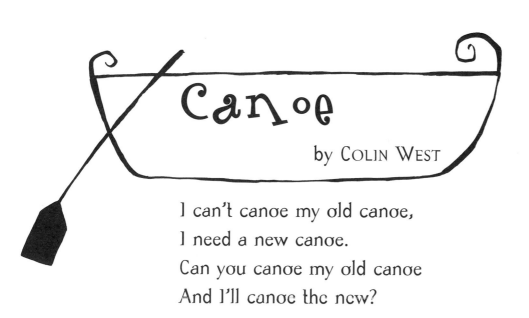

Canoe

by COLIN WEST

I can't canoe my old canoe,
I need a new canoe.
Can you canoe my old canoe
And I'll canoe the new?

A Magic Tent

by GERARD BENSON

Inside this tent
The world is different.
Balls thrown in the air
Stay there;
They spin from hand to hand
And never land.

The lovely lady in sparkling tights
Flies like a bird between the lights,
Now gold, now twinkling blue,
Now red, now every rainbow hue.
Before our very eyes
She changes colour as she flies.

High on a wire a fat man dances
And way below a pony prances,
Carrying a girl with a spangly shirt
And floating ballet skirt,
Who stands up proud
On one foot, blowing kisses to the crowd.
It's impossible! It's magical!!

Only the clowns tumble and fall.
With their strange noses and their enormous shoes,
They trip; then rise again: they never really lose.
While drums kerthump and trumpets flare and blare,
We stare, just stare,
At this Otherworld of wonderment.

And if they whisked the top off this fantastic tent,
Would everything be quite the same
As when we came?
Would we
Look up and see
The sky, that old familiar blue?
Or something new?
A Universe new-made, where dogs and cats
And Aunts and Uncles swing like acrobats,
With girls and boys, and even their Mas and Pas,
On heavenly trapezes, slung from the moon and stars?*!

53

A Rainbow by her Chair

by ADÈLE GERAS

My Nana looks at jumpers greedily.
She doesn't see the garment you've got on.
She knitted it, but that's not relevant.
She's busy re-inventing: thinking how
the wool might look when put alongside blue
or brown or white or that amazing pink
that's lying in her basket. Some fat ball
that used to be a cardigan or scarf
is wound up, ready to be something new;
to reappear as stripes or squares or socks
or teacosies, or lacy coats for dolls,
or pull-on hats which make it look as though
your head has sprouted moss-stitch overnight.

Her eager scissors make a tiny snip
in what was once the ribbing. One sharp pull
and rows of plain and purl and purl and plain
in fancy combinations, disappear,
and Nana winds them up until she's got
a woolly rainbow waiting by her chair.

She takes the silver knitting needles out
and starts transforming: click and pause and click.

My Dad is a Rock and Roller

by Tony Bradman

My dad is a rock and roller,
My mum is a disco queen;
Brother Keith's a crazy drummer,
He's the *wildest* that you've seen!

Sister Dionne is a singer,
With our cousin, Peggy Sue;
Uncle Paul, well he's a showman,
There's not much that he can't do.

Auntie Tammy is a cowgirl,
Grandpa plays a mean guitar;
Grandma is an opera singer,
Now she's terrific – what a star!

Every week we get together,
Man we really have a ball.
And me? I'm just a brand new baby.
BUT I'M THE LOUDEST OF THEM ALL!

Red Shoes

by OPAL PALMER ADISA

When I saw them
in the magazine
I knew I had to have them.
Red shoes
with tiny bows on the back
and straps that formed an X.

They were the shoes
I had been dreaming of
red shoes to dance and skip
and jump and hop in
pretty red shoes.

Please mummy, pretty please
Can I have them?
May I have these red shoes?
Shiny shoes
that are just my size.
Please, pretty please
Can I have these red shoes
these shoes that say put me on?

I wear them out the store
and once home
I run and show
them to my friends.

I slept in them that first night.
I skipped in them all the next day.
I danced on my tippy toes
I even climbed a tree in them.
After a week my red shoes
didn't look new any more
but I still loved them.
My first red shoes!

Ode to my oldest Best Shoes

by Kwame Dawes

Soft and just the right shape too,
my feet slip in, my toes are giggling,
they know how to make a ball swerve
they get green with grass
and brown with mud
and black with soot
and wet with rain
and smelly and grey
and still feel as right as can be

There is no sweating or straining
no moaning and groaning
to get my feet to slip right in
It's as if I am floating
or dancing a jig
barefoot in cotton
through nettles and thorns
through garbage heaps
over nails and glass
and still feel as right as can be.

That's why I am crying like a baby
and limping like a jalopy truck
that is why my toes are whining
that they can't breathe or laugh at all
no dirt, no dust
no stones in the toes
no paint and grease
no games in the bush
I'll never feel right again, Mum,
not with these awful new shoes, Mum,
not with these awful new shoes!

Brand New – and Bust!

by Simon Rae

It worked yesterday;
It doesn't work today.

I'm sure it wasn't my fault.
I wasn't mucking about.
I don't remember dropping it:
I didn't leave it out.

I read all the instructions
(Well, half-way down page 3).
I'm doing exactly what it says
And it's not working – See?

I really didn't force it
or over-wind the spring.
I didn't shake it upside down
I didn't do *anything*.

It worked yesterday;
It doesn't work today.

I didn't get sand in it.
I didn't get it wet.
I didn't put it in the microwave
As part of a silly bet.

I didn't let the dog have it
Or give the baby a go,
And when Gary pleaded for a turn,
I just said No!

It worked yesterday;
It doesn't work today.

Other people's are all right —
It simply isn't fair.
I bet that when we take it back
They'll say Beyond Repair.

I say Brand New - and BUST!

My Car's Reward

by SOPHIE HANNAH

Speedometers don't fix themselves,
Not of their own accord
But my car's did. It hadn't moved
For months and then it soared
Suddenly, sparing me repairs
That I could not afford.
One day a garage of its own
Will be my car's reward.

If life were fair, my car would win
The world's best car award.
My car has got a lot of friends:
Three Audis and a Ford.
If it spends too much time alone
My car, like most, gets bored
But with a garage of its own
A car feels reassured.

A brand new garage of its own,
A garage squat and broad,
A garage like a little home,
Red-bricked and metal-doored,
From which my car can come and go
While other cars applaud,
That nobody can take away
Will be my car's reward.

My House

by LAURENCE LERNER

I had a house for seven years:
I must have climbed the stair
Five thousand times; and every day
Locked and unlocked the door.
It watched me clean my teeth, and wash
My face, and brush my hair.

And then I went away, and so
Put up my house to let,
"Just think," I said, "of all the lovely
Money I will get."
A stranger known as Mr Jones
Came to live in it.

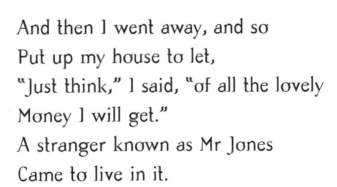

A year went by; and I came back,
And all I brought was new:
New shoes, new suit, new suitcase too,
New plans for what I'd do.
But when I put my latchkey in,
My house said, "Who are you?"

A Short Hop to a Habitat Swap

by BRIAN MOSES

You've heard about changing rooms,
well, why can't animals do it too?
Dolphin swap with eagle,
penguin with kangaroo.

Polar bear offers snow hole,
gorilla quits jungle den,
camel gives up the desert
for a home in a Scottish glen.

Termites leave their mounds
for a coral reef under the sea.
A mole grown tired of a hole
is fixing a nest in a tree.

Badger offers his burrow
to a lobster and a crab,
but who would want to swap places
with a slug sleeping under a slab?

Or a spider who offers a web
but doesn't say when he's leaving?
Well, it could turn out to be true
but it all takes some believing.

Animals changing habitats –
it might catch on at the zoo,
every year, when spring comes round,
old homes being swapped for new.

Cow and Cat

by JOHN AGARD

Cow and Cat
went a-wooing
and needless to say
romance was brewing.

Something old something new
something borrowed something blue.
Bless my whiskers bless my horn
love between the two was born.

And so it came to pass
that under a sky
of wedly June
Cow said Moo

and Cat said Mew
and vicar Owl
with furrowed brow
said too-hoo too-hoo.

And all around
the forest chapel
the air cast its spell
of sweet "I do. I do."

First Lamb

by GILLIAN CLARKE

First lamb, born under Mars
and Venus and all the stars.
A ewe and her lamb in the dark,
new-born. When she talks
in her soft, growly voice, he echoes.
When I carry him home, she follows
from the field to the warm, dry shed,
hay, fresh water, a clean straw bed.
She's in love with his cry, his taste, his smell,
the lovable, lickable, salt-sea smell
of the baby she carried inside her, curled,
to be born tonight in a starry world.

Next Door's Cat

by Valerie Bloom

Next door's cat is by the pond
Sitting, waiting for the fish,
Next door's cat thinks Geraldine
Would make a tasty dish.

He's had Twinkle and Rose Red,
He ate Alberta too,
And all we found were Junior's bones
When that horrid cat was through.

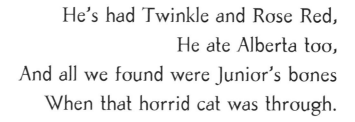

Next door's cat comes round at night,
Strikes when we're in bed,
In the morning when we wake
Another fish is dead.

Next door's cat has seen the new fish,
He thinks that it's a goner,
What a surprise he's going to get,
When he finds it's a piranha.

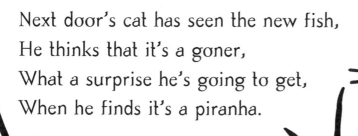

Tabby

by GRACE NICHOLS

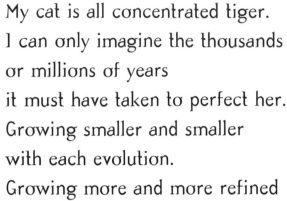

My cat is all concentrated tiger.
I can only imagine the thousands
or millions of years
it must have taken to perfect her.
Growing smaller and smaller
with each evolution.
Growing more and more refined
and even-tempered under her fur.

See how she constantly licks
and grooms herself all over?

A small Queen of Sheba
stamping everywhere her padded
signature – a royal reminder
of the days she was full-blown tiger.
Older O much older than Egypt.

Now, just look at her – my grey
and black tabby, stepping lightly,
emerging head first, from between the green
garden stalks –

Ancient and new as the birth of a star.

Mister-Ry

by James Berry

Wild New-Forest Pony takes my apple.
Eats my banana too. Looks for more.
I stroke him. He follows me. So strangely
friendly towards me, he makes
me suddenly name him, Mister-Ry! And, more:
next morning shocks me out of bed.
Arched back on long legs and long neck
crops grass, in our front garden. I
rush out calling MISTER-RY! MISTER-RY!
In a low rumble of a neigh, he comes —
long face pushing, nuzzling me.
Our dog, Worrier, dashes about,
teasing Mister-Ry to play with him.
Picking him up, I put Worrier lying
flat on the back of the horse. All
on his own he walks with dog rider
round and round the garden. Then, my go.
Holding neck and mane, I climb up,
sit erect, having my trotting ride
round the garden, when, along my
streetside, a blast of applause shakes me
and goes on through my barebacked ride,
never stopping. I say, Okay Mister-Ry.

Sharp, sharp, he stops. I dismount,
looking. I see the Queen. Clapping too
the Queen is there, saying to me:
Give him a drink now. Give him a drink.
I run into the house. Get a bucket
of water. Come back with it, panting
with new disbelief.

    No horse is there.

       No audience is there.
In the far, far distance I hear
wild clattering of hoofs going,

    going away —

       till all is quiet.

Biscuit

by SIMON RAE

Biscuit came in a tin,
Biscuits often do.
But this Biscuit
          wasn't a biscuit;
He was a puppy!
He thought everything was a present,
Because he was a present himself.
He bounced up and down
And he bounced round the room,
He bounced at the balloons
But when he landed on top
They didn't bounce back
They simply went
          POP!!
And everyone laughed,
Biscuit laughed too. *Arrph! arrph!*
Biscuit liked everything.
Biscuit licked everybody.
Biscuit looked everywhere –
Was there a present for Biscuit?

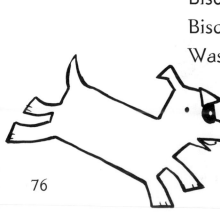

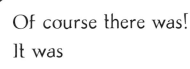

Of course there was!
It was
        a biscuit!
"Good dog, Biscuit."
Mmmm, good dog-biscuit,
thought Biscuit.
Biscuit buried his present under the chair,
Then he pretended
It wasn't there.
It was his new trick.
Biscuit barked. Biscuit begged.
Then he whisked round and round
Through everyone's legs.
Up and down
Round and round
Faster and faster . . .
No one could catch him
Or trap him or grab him
Biscuit was so excited
He just couldn't stop
Until
        Oh dear!
Disaster!

"Bad dog, Biscuit!"
Sad dog, Biscuit.
"Dear, sweet Biscuit."
Everyone loved Biscuit,
Loved him to bits.
They hugged him and stroked him
And tickled his ears
Until Biscuit felt dopey
And dozey and droopy.
He found his old tin
And climbed back in.
"Good night, Biscuit,
Sleep tight."

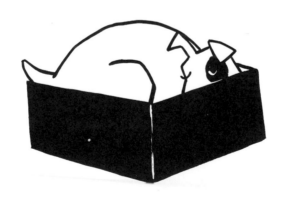

Doggerel

by Jeni Townsend

One, Two, what shall I do?
The dog's run off with my new shoe.

Three, Four, out the door
He's done this kind of thing before.

Five, Six, get in a fix
He thinks it's one of his party tricks.

Seven, Eight, in a right old state
He's nipped out under the garden gate.

Nine, Ten, I don't know when
I'll ever get it back again!

Dog to the Rescue

(for Jim and Diana)

by PENELOPE SHUTTLE

Her eyes are big and bright
as dog stars.

Her coat is black with white stars,
or white with black stars.

She is a dog who looks on the bright side.
A cheer-up dog.
A maybe-it-won't-happen dog.

Is that mascara on her long long eyelashes?
Will she be on the cover of Dog Vogue?

From an animal shelter
She has come to live in a house
where everyone was sad.

Now they stop feeling sad.
And when people say:
Oh you are not looking sad any more,

they say:

No, it is because
Ellie the new Rescue Dog has rescued us.

Who Polishes the Moon?

by JOHN LYONS

I wonder who polishes the moon
to make it shine like a new silver spoon.

My big brother says
the sun does when we are not looking;
then quickly hides
on the other side of the world.

I think he is kidding me.

Foreday Mornin

by JOHN LYONS

A new day,
a cool day
before de blazin sun come,
wen grass still wettin meh feet.

Foreday mornin
wen Goleye Sarah
pickin ripe sapodilla
wid bright yella beak.

Foreday mornin
a noisy new day
wen de old cock Rufus
crow in de yard
an ripe mango still fallin
"buddup" down hard.

Foreday mornin
wen Granma wake me up.
"Get up, get up,
early birds get de worms."

But I want mango.

Old Day, New Day

by TONY MITTON

Old day, gold day,
where did you go?

Over the skyline,
sinking low.
Into the arms
of the waiting night
to nestle myself
in its dark delight.

New day, blue day,
what will you bring?

Light in the sky
and a song to sing.
Sun bobs brightly
up with the dawn:
Hope in the heart
as the day is born.

84

The Sundial Hat

by ROGER MCGOUGH

Standing in the garden
I have no idea what time it is
even though I am wearing
the sundial hat you gave me

It is a lovely morning
what with the sun etc,
and I won't hear a word
said against it

What the scene requires
is an aural dimension
and, chuffed to high heaven
birds provide it

How best to describe this day?
New? OK. New. New. New.

The New Soca Beat

by ALEXANDER D. GREAT

I want to be
Near to the sea,
Under the shade of a coconut tree,
On a Caribbean isle,
In a tropical trance,
Where the sunbeams smile
And the steel drums dance.

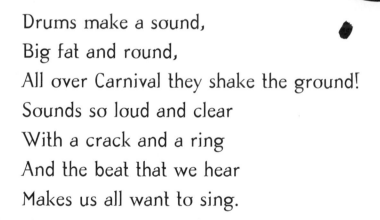

Drums make a sound,
Big fat and round,
All over Carnival they shake the ground!
Sounds so loud and clear
With a crack and a ring
And the beat that we hear
Makes us all want to sing.

Let me explain
Simple and plain
Just what that Soca Beat is, once again.
We dance in the street
When it's Carnival Day
And the New Soca Beat
Is the beat the bands play.

Chook a-chook a-chook
In the humming-bird heat,
Ba-dum, ba-dum
hear the New Soca Beat,
Bra-ba-dap, bra-dap,
So sharp and so neat
That you shimmy in your seat
To the New Soca Beat.

You can't stop me!

by MIRIAM MOSS

High up in the heather
where nobody was,
and no noise was, but birdsong,
and nothing moved, but the breeze,
something new began.

First a ripple
then a gurgle
and a small snake of water
spilled its way downhill.
"You can't stop me,"
burbled the little brook,
"Not now, not ever . . . never."
And it chattered its way
over pebbles
down waterfalls
past cows
into a splashing stream . . .
"You can't stop me,"
sang the stream,
"Not now, not ever . . . never."

It swished
it swirled
through willows
round fishermen
past swans
into a rolling river . . .
"YOU CAN'T STOP ME!"
chanted the rolling river,
"NOT NOW, NOT EVER . . . NEVER!"
It flounced
it flowed
under bridges
round barges
past smokestacks
into a swollen river . . .
"YOU CAN'T STOP ME!"
swelled the swollen river,
"NOT NOW, NOT EVER . . . NEVER!"

It bulged
it slid
past walkers
under gulls
to bobbing boats
and the swaying sea . . .
"YOU CAN'T STOP ME!"
roared the mighty river.
"NOT NOW, NOT EVER . . .
NEVER!"

"Oh, Hush," said the sea,
as it swallowed it up.

The Sea's Hands

by GEORGE SZIRTES

The sea lays big glass hands on the sand,
spreading its fingers out as if new
to the shore. It can't quite believe in it.
It wants to hold on before the glass breaks.

And it does break, giggling with froth,
so it lets go and slips back as it always knew
it would, and the waves clap their hands
erupting broad cream flakes

of pleasure into the air which is moving
and will move for ever, through
anyone's fingers. And the sea doesn't mind.
It is the glass, not the heart, that breaks.

At Enniscrone

by UNA LEAVY

The beach sweeps long and bare
at Enniscrone,
waves lap and dash
against the glassy stones.

I shape a sandcastle,
my hands are cold;
sea sneakers reach my feet —
I scream and run.

And Daddy laughs!
He tosses my new kite,
it sulks and dives
then almost soars from sight.

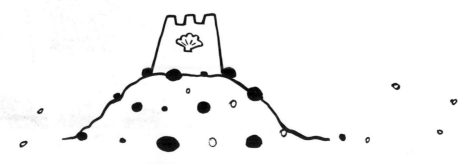

The salty wind
is bristling on our cheeks
and marram grass
leans flat above the beach.

We scan the shore for treasures
from the deep,
but there is nothing here
for us to keep

except this April day
at Enniscrone
when all the world belongs
to us alone.

The Stane in the Fish in the Boat in the bay

by JOHN RICE

Oot in the bay,
the pearl-grey bay
there's an auld fisher boat
a-rockin', a-rockin',
a-rockin' a' the fair-weather day
in the pearl-grey bay.

In the auld fisher boat
that will ever aye float
there's a ticht green net
a-stretchin', a-stretchin',
a-stretchin' like a wee kitten's coat
in the auld fisher boat.

In the ticht green net
that's ever aye wet
there's a siller-blue fish
a-wrigglin', a-wrigglin',
a-wrigglin' in a fast dance set
in the ticht green net.

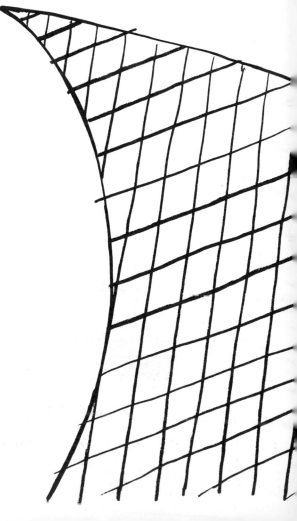

In the siller-blue fish
that will grant ony wish
there's a mottled moonstane
a-gleamin', a-gleamin',
a-gleamin' like a bone china dish
in the siller-blue fish.

In the mottled moonstane
as bright as sheep-bane
there's a pearl-grey bay
a-sparklin', a-sparklin',
a-sparklin' like a star a' alane
in the mottled moonstane.

Oot in the bay
the pearl-grey bay
there's a new fisher boat
a-rockin', a-rockin',
a-rockin' a' the fair-weather day
in the pearl-grey bay.

Only the Bones of the Dinosaurs

by GERALDINE MCCAUGHREAN

Left only the bones of the dinosaurs,
We cannot tell today
What colour their hides were, their outsides were,
So we paint them grey
Or brown, or muddy green, or tan.
But who are we to say
They didn't go round in purple skins
Or pink as peachy trees;
Crimson-crested and scarlet-scaled
Or blue as tropical seas,
With armour-plate of flashing zinc
On their gigantic knees?

Picture with bilious tricorn horns
A puce triceratops,
Iridescent pterosaurs,
Or, like ocelots,
Mammoths with mazy, golden pelts
And jet black spots.

We paint them grimly awaiting their end,
Drably camouflage-clad
To blend in with a mouldering fate
Inescapably bad.
But what if their views were rainbow bright,
And only *ours* are drab?

Oh, to see old beasts with new eyes.

Newts

by GILLIAN CLARKE

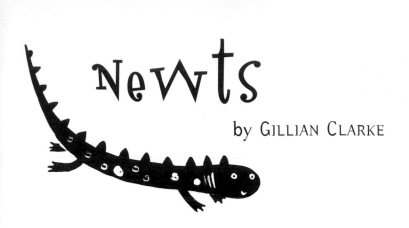

Dinosaur-dreamers! Hibernators!
Under stones, under sacks of potatoes,
fast asleep all winter you hunker
deep down under the coal in the bunker.

Then we come along with shovel and hod
to plunder your wonderful city. We tread
with great care, and then, one by one,
we lift you into the new spring sun.

You're sleepy as children on daddy's shoulder
when nights were darker and days were colder.
But wake up! Warm up! Time to be stirring.
Spring is here and the whole world's purring.

100

Old Soldier

by BRENDAN KENNELLY

"I'm eighty-eight," he said,
    trenchtwinkle in his eyes,
"and though I fought in the worst o' wars
    I'm barkin' lively.

Slogged in the Kimberley Diamond Mines,
    sang on Fiddler's Green
and never, never would accept
    the notion of a has-been.

The years are old, my heart is young,
    there's plenty left to do;
strings of a fiddle, words of a song
    keep me feelin' new.

Complainin' gets ya nowhere.
    Old eyes need a sparklin' sight.
Take me for a walk, young friend,
    to see the Shannon light."

What She Knew

by BRIAN PATTEN

"Give me something new," she said.
I said, "Surely if I do
Soon after possessing it
You'd say it's no longer new."

"Then give me something old," she said.
I said, "Surely if I do
Because you have not seen it yet
To you it would be new."

"Sometimes new is old," she said,
"And sometimes old is new."
"New is in the mind," I said,
She said she knew that too.

old couples

by GEORGE SZIRTES

Some lighter than leaves
Some wrinkled as water,
And each of them once
Was a son or a daughter.

Their mothers and fathers
Were children in turn,
Like water that dries,
Like leaves that must burn.

And here I stand waiting,
I'm still good as new,
My leaves are just grown
And I'm shiny with dew.

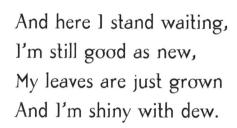

To be here at all
Is a reason for wonder
With so much to come
And so much gone under.

The Seventy-five O'Clock News

by GERALDINE MCCAUGHREAN

They should find a new name for the News
For the more I watch it, the more it looks
Like shiny postcards of the same old views,
Like new dust-jackets on familiar books.

The selfsame stories come hurtling round
Like comets in their ellipse:
The selfsame people, the selfsame sounds;
The same pictures dubbed with new scripts.

Floods, disasters, famines and wars;
The same crimes, the same scandal and lies;
The same hissed whispers behind the same doors,
Like the buzzing of numberless flies.

The news I would choose would leap from the screen.
With "Hold the front page!" and a "Scoop!"
It would fill whole journals and magazines,
And make jaded news-vendors whoop.

"A megatomic explosion of peace!
Twelve angels caught on radar!
The discovery, by metal-detecting geese
Of a Mesopatamian railcar!
Volcano swallows locust swarm!
Hailstorm of phoenix eggs!

Whole forests migrate in search of the warm;
And they're smuggling laughter, in kegs.
There's a permanent, poppy-red cure for the blues
For which mermaids are quitting the sea.
Read all about it!" Here is the news:
The news you would choose to see.

Instead of these seeming déjà vus,
Here is the seventy-five o'clock news.

De

by Valerie Bloom

De snow, de sleet, de lack o' heat,
De wishy-washy sunlight,
De lip turn blue, de cold, "ACHOO!"
De runny nose, de frostbite,

De creakin' knee, de misery,
De joint dem all rheumatic,
De icy bed, (de blanket dead)
De burs' pipe in de attic.

De window a-shake, de glass near break,
De wind dat cut like razor,
De wonderin' why you never buy
De window from dat double-glazer.

De thick new coat, zip to the throat,
De nose an' ears all pinky,
De weepin' sky, de clothes can't dry,
De days dem long an' inky.

De icy road, de heavy load,
De las' minute Christmus shoppin'
De cuss an' fret 'cause you feget
De ribbon an' de wrappin'.

De mud, de grime, de slush, de slime,
De place gloomy since November,
De sinkin' heart, is jus' de start, o'
De wintertime,
December.

This poem was inspired by Thomas Hood's poem *No.*

Snowed-on Song

by MICHAEL HOROVITZ

In the garden square where
the neighbourhood children
play every day
there suddenly stands
a strange new presence;
the wholly

        snow

           man

— see how he stares
with stoned eyes,
no ears
to speak of
— jagg'd
teeth of ice,
his nose a lumpen icicle
— and snow

        drops

          all

            around

– opening the secret
hearts of snowdrops
to think about
opening out
their infant petals
into teenage
                    torches
            and lamps

– while tall fir trees
bask in the cask
of their new fur hats,
(made from imaginary,
not real animal fur),
and their Viking helmets,
moustaches
            and beards
                    of snow.

– and when at a bitterly
sharp gust of wind
snowman wobbles, half
                    falls
and begins to weep for pain

— the children pat his cheeks,
dry his tears
and little hands build him

> up again

— and up he stays

— till bedtime
when the snowed-on scene
begins
> to end
> in rain.

That Time of Year
(or New Year Resolutions)

by TRACEY BLANCE

Keep my bedroom tidy,
Share my sweets with friends;
Save up all my money
Instead of spend spend spend.

Or shall I

Leave my bedroom messy,
Eat chocolates by the ton,
Spend all my money?
That sounds MUCH more fun!

Our Traveller, Underground

by NICKI JACKOWSKA

A seed underground
doesn't know what
its name will be
how it will feel
for light to travel along
its stem; not yet.

Curled like a woodlouse
the sprout is white as bone
not ready for battle
through earth and stone
the breakaway from home.

It doesn't give up, our
traveller, knocking the lid
of the world until
it breaks. We watch
from above as grains of soil

crumble, shiver and shift
to let it through
jump and dance in delight
as two green flags uncurl
from a single stem
twin faces to the new raw light.

A New Me

by MATTHEW SWEENEY

What's all this about a new me
to go with the new century?
I'm quite happy with the me I am.
So what if my room's a mess
and I watch all the TV I can!
I could be into cat-murders,
or running away to Paris,
or burning the school down.

I'd like a new you, and a new Dad,
a pair who wouldn't fight,
who'd treat me like a friend,
and who'd lose the no-gooders
who are always hanging around.
I'd like you to quit smoking,
and be mean to the bottle-bank.
I'd like Dad to join a gym,
but I keep all this to myself —
in fact, I'm quite prepared to
contemplate an amnesty
and let the two of you be
but only if the year 2000
makes you change your tune to me.

115

Bug

by WENDY COPE

Here I come, the millennium bug,
I'm hairy and scary, a six-legged thug,

A horrible monster, a wrecker, a killer,
Who'll do far more harm than King Kong or Godzilla,

Or so people think. But I could prove them wrong.
I'm doing my best and I haven't got long.

There's only one reason why I am a threat –
Though I work hard at numbers, there's one I forget.

1990
1991
1992 1993
1994 1995
1996 1997

I can count to a thousand and go higher still.
Another nine hundred and more and I'm brill,

But then there's a problem. I ransack my mind.
The number you need is the one I can't find.

I'm struggling to learn it before the New Year.
My case isn't hopeless, so be of good cheer.

I may just recall, as you sing Auld Lang Syne,
The number that comes after one nine nine nine.

1998
1999

Bright New World

by FAUSTIN CHARLES

Let us make a world
Where everything is new
Where sorrows are few
Where the young respect the old.

Let us shine a new sun
Make all bright days into one
And silver the heavens with fun.

Let us make a new start
Swell the joy in each heart;
Cast out wrongs, make new rights
And never get caught putting out lights.

Old World, New World

by JOHN AGARD

Spices and gold once cast a spell
on bearded men in caravels.

New World New World – cried history
Old World Old World – sighed every tree.

But Indian tribes long long ago
had sailed this archipelago.

They who were used to flutes of bone
translated talk of wind on stone

Yet their feathered tongues were drowned
when Discovery beat its drum.

New World New World – spices and gold
Old World Old World – the legends told.

New World New World – cried history
Old World Old World – sighed every tree.

First Journey

by MAURA DOOLEY

A pale new moon,
A starry sky,
The tail of a comet
Streams by.

A bud unfurls,
A baby's fist,
This winter morning,
Sunkissed.

An open door
Into the light,
A heart's first journey.
Hold tight!

The sun, the moon,
The stars all sing,
A new life's calling.
Begin!

Future Past

by LAVINIA GREENLAW

Now, look back. Follow

Every star from the moment

When its light was born.

121

Index of Poems and Poets

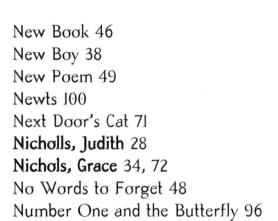

Index of Poems and Poets

Acknowledgements

A New Blue Bike © John Rice 2000; A Magic Tent © Gerard Benson 2000; A New Me © Matthew Sweeney 2000; A Rainbow by Her Chair © Adèle Geras 2000; A Short Hop to a Habitat Swap © Brian Moses 2000; A Walk Through Yourself © Brendan Kennelly 2000; After the Storm © Opal Palmer Adisa 2000; Archibald, Marjorie, Otto: Cuckoo! © Mark Hewitt 2000; At Enniscrone © Una Leavy 2000; Before the Ball © John Agard 2000; Biscuit © Simon Rae 2000; Brand New – and Bust! © Simon Rae 2000; Bright New World © Faustin Charles 2000; Broomstick Ballet © John Agard 2000; Bug © Wendy Cope 2000; But is There New In It? © John Mole 2000; Canoe © Colin West 2000; Cow and Cat © John Agard 2000; De © Valerie Bloom 2000; Doggerel © Jeni Townsend 2000; Dog to the Rescue © Penelope Shuttle 2000; First Journey © Maura Dooley 2000; First Lamb © Gillian Clarke 2000; Foreday Mornin © John Lyons 2000; Future Past © Lavinia Greenlaw 2000; Glitterbread © Brian Moses 2000; Haven't a Clue © Dave Calder 2000; I Love Johnnie Bake © John Lyons 2000; Keeping My Own Company © Opal Adisa 2000; Kicking Through the New © Grace Nichols 2000; Mister-Ry © James Berry 2000; My Car's Reward © Sophie Hannah 2000; My Dad is a Rock and Roller © Tony Bradman 2000; My House © Laurence Lerner 2000; New Book © Tony Mitton 2000; New Boy © Peter Sansom 2000; New Poem © Roger McGough 2000; Newts © Gillian Clarke 2000; Next Door's Cat © Valerie Bloom 2000; No Words to Forget © Ian McMillan 2000; Number One and the Butterfly © U.A. Fanthorpe 2000; Ode to My Oldest Best Shoes © Kwame Dawes 2000; Old Couples © George Szirtes 2000; Old Day, New Day © Tony Mitton 2000; Old Soldier © Brendan Kennelly 2000; Old Tongue © Jackie Kay 2000; Old World, New World © John Agard 2000; Only The Bones of the Dinosaurs © Geraldine McCaughrean 2000; Our Traveller, Underground © Nicki Jackowska 2000; Red Shoes © Opal Palmer Adisa 2000; Roses Round My Door © Geraldine McCaughrean 2000; Seventeen Things To Do With a Baby © Judith Nicholls 2000; Smiles Like Roses © Helen Dunmore 2000; Snowed-on Song © Michael Horovitz 2000; Tabby © Grace Nichols 2000; That Time of Year © Tracey Blance 2000; The Magic of New Notebooks © Bill Lewis 2000; The Mucky Princess © Adrian Mitchell 2000; The New Soca Beat © Alexander D. Great 2000; The Rain's Feet © George Szirtes 2000; The Sea's Hands © George Szirtes 2000; The Seventy five O'Clock News © Geraldine McCaughrean 2000; The Stane in the Fish in the Boat in the Bay © John Rice 2000; The Sundial Hat © Roger McGough 2000; The Thing © Gareth Owen 2000; Three © Carol Ann Duffy 2000; Wishes to Welcome Two New Babies © Adrian Mitchell 2000; What's New? © John Mole 2000; What She Knew © Brian Patten 2000; Who Polishes the Moon? © John Lyons 2000; Who Wants To Be a Dragonfly? © Laurence Lerner 2000; You Can't Stop Me! © Miriam Moss 2000.

The following poems have been published elsewhere since being commissioned for this book: De by Valerie Bloom which appeared in Time's Tiding, published by Anvil Press in 1999 and Old Soldier by Brendan Kennelly which appeared in his collection Begin, published by Bloodaxe Books in 1999.

With New poems by

Gerard Benson

Tracey Blance

Tony Bradman

Faustin Charles

Wendy Cope

Maura Dooley

Helen Dunmore

Adèle Geras

Lavinia Greenlaw

Mark Hewitt

Nicki Jackowska

Brendan Kennelly

Laurence Lerner

John Lyons

Roger McGough

Adrian Mitchell

John Mole

Miriam Moss

Grace Nichols

Opal Palmer Adisa

Simon Rae

Peter Sansom

Matthew Sweeney

Jeni Townsend

John Agard

James Berry

Valerie Bloom

Dave Calder

Gillian Clarke

Kwame Dawes

Carol Ann Duffy

U. A. Fanthorpe

Alexander D. Great

Sophie Hannah

Michael Horovitz

Jackie Kay

Una Leavy

Bill Lewis

Geraldine McCaughrean

Ian McMillan

Tony Mitton

Brian Moses

Judith Nicholls

Gareth Owen

Brian Patten

John Rice

Penelope Shuttle

George Szirtes

Colin West